TECHNICALITY OF CLIMATE CHANGE

JONATHAN WILLIE

TABLE OF CONTENT

Writing a book on such a complex and multifaceted issue as climate change would not have been possible without the help and support of many people.

First and foremost, I would like to thank the countless scientists and researchers who have dedicated their lives to studying and understanding climate change. Their work forms the foundation of this book, and I am deeply grateful for their contributions.

I would also like to thank my editor and publisher for their guidance and support throughout the writing process. Their suggestions and insights helped to shape the book into its final form.

I am also grateful to my family and friends for their unwavering support and encouragement. Their belief in me and this project kept me going through the many challenges of writing a book.

Finally, I would like to acknowledge the importance of the readers. It is my hope that this book will serve as a valuable resource for individuals, communities, and policy-makers, and will contribute to the efforts of tackling the climate change.

Thank you all for your support and contribution

PREFACE

Climate change is one of the most pressing issues facing our planet today. The overwhelming scientific consensus is that human activity, specifically the burning of fossil fuels and deforestation, is causing the Earth's climate to warm at an unprecedented rate.

This warming is leading to a host of negative consequences, including more frequent and severe heat waves, droughts, and storms, as well as rising sea levels that threaten to inundate low-lying areas.

In this book, we delve into the scientific evidence for climate change, examining both the causes and the potential impacts. We also explore the various policy options that are available to us, from reducing greenhouse gas emissions to adapting to the changes that are already happening.

Our goal is to provide readers with a comprehensive understanding of this complex and critical issue, so that they can make informed decisions about how to respond to the challenges of climate change.

Climate change is not just an environmental issue, it is also a social, economic, and political issue, and it is one that affects us all. It is therefore important that we all become better informed about this issue and that we work together to find solutions. This book is a starting point for that journey.

INTRODUCTION

Climate change refers to long-term shifts in temperature, precipitation, wind patterns, and other indicators of the Earth's climate.

These shifts can be natural, but human activity, such as burning fossil fuels and deforestation, is a major contributor to climate change. As a result of climate change, the Earth's average temperature has been increasing, and there have been more frequent and severe weather events, such as heatwaves, droughts, and storms.

The impacts of climate change can be felt on a local, regional, and global scale, and they can have serious consequences for human health, agriculture, and the environment.

Climate change refers to the long-term changes in the Earth's climate, particularly changes in temperature and precipitation patterns. The issue of climate change has become increasingly important in recent years, as scientists have observed rising temperatures, melting ice caps, and other changes that are thought to be the result of human activities, such as the burning of fossil fuels and deforestation.

Many books have been written about climate change, covering a wide range of topics, from the science behind climate change, to the impacts of climate change on society and the environment, to potential solutions for reducing greenhouse gas emissions and slowing the rate of global warming.

Some notable books on climate change include "The Uninhabitable Earth" by David Wallace-Wells, "Climate Wars" by Gwynne Dyer, "The Sixth Extinction" by Elizabeth Kolbert, "Climate of Hope" by Michael Bloomberg and Carl Pope, and "Drawdown" edited by Paul Hawken.

Overview of climate change and its causes

Climate change refers to the long-term changes in the Earth's climate, particularly changes in temperature and precipitation patterns.

The primary cause of climate change is the burning of fossil fuels, such as coal, oil, and natural gas, which releases greenhouse gases (primarily carbon dioxide) into the atmosphere.

These gases trap heat from the sun, causing the Earth's surface to warm up. This process is known as the greenhouse effect.

Other human activities also contribute to climate change, including deforestation, which reduces the amount of carbon absorbed by trees and other vegetation, and agriculture and livestock farming, which produce methane and other greenhouse gases.

The burning of fossil fuels and other human activities have caused the levels of carbon dioxide and other greenhouse gases in the atmosphere to rise rapidly in recent decades, leading to an increase in the Earth's average surface temperature.

Climate change has a wide range of impacts, including rising sea levels, more frequent and severe heat waves, more intense storms, and changes in precipitation patterns, which can lead to droughts and flooding.

These changes can have significant consequences for human society and the natural environment, including impacts on food security, human health, and biodiversity.

CHAPTER 1

THE IMPACT OF CLIMATE CHANGE

Climate change has a wide range of impacts, both on the natural environment and on human society. Some of the most notable impacts include:

1. Rising sea levels: As the Earth's temperature increases, ice caps and glaciers are melting, causing sea levels to rise.

This can lead to coastal flooding and erosion, and can also contaminate ground water and saltwater intrusion which affects freshwater resources.

2.   Increased frequency and severity of extreme weather events: Climate change can lead to more frequent and severe heat waves, droughts, floods, and storms.

These events can cause widespread damage to infrastructure, homes, and businesses, and can also lead to food and water shortages.

3   Impacts on agriculture and food security: Changes in temperature and precipitation patterns can make it more difficult for farmers to grow crops, and can also lead to pests and diseases spreading to new areas.

This can affect food security, particularly in developing countries, where many people depend on farming for their livelihoods.

4   Impacts on biodiversity: Climate change can cause species to migrate to new areas or to become extinct, as they are not able to adapt to the changing conditions.

This can disrupt ecosystems and can also affect the services that ecosystems provide, such as pollination, pest control, and water purification.

5   Health impacts: Climate change can affect air and water quality and can also increase the spread of disease. This can lead to respiratory and cardiovascular diseases, heat stroke and heat exhaustion, and other health problems.

1. Economic impacts: Climate change can affect industries such as agriculture, fishing, and tourism, and can also lead to increased costs for infrastructure and emergency services. This can have a significant impact on economic growth and development.

2. Social impacts: Climate change can lead to displacement of people due to rising sea levels, floods, drought, and other extreme weather events. It can also have a disproportionate impact on vulnerable populations, including low-income communities, women, children and indigenous people.

Effect of climate change on human society

Climate change has a wide range of impacts on human society, including effects on health, infrastructure, and access to resources. Rising temperatures can lead to increased incidence of heat stroke and other heat-related illnesses, as well as worsen air quality.

Extreme weather events such as floods, droughts, and storms can damage or destroy infrastructure and disrupt transportation and access to clean water. Changes in precipitation patterns can affect crop yields and lead to food insecurity. Climate change also has the potential to exacerbate existing social and economic inequalities.

Where does the hope of human lies on the issue of climate change?

The hope for addressing the issue of climate change lies in the ability of humanity to reduce greenhouse gas emissions through the implementation of sustainable technologies and practices, and the adoption of policies to limit the use of fossil fuels.

Additionally, international cooperation and the participation of individuals, businesses, and governments will be necessary to effectively address the issue.

Will man and the planet last for another hundred years if the issues of climate change persist?

It is difficult to predict with certainty what the state of the planet will be in 100 years if the issue of climate change persists. However, it is widely agreed among scientists that if we do not take significant action to reduce greenhouse gas emissions and mitigate the effects of climate change, the consequences could be severe.

This could include more frequent and intense heatwaves, droughts, and storms, as well as rising sea levels and increased risk of extinction of many species.

Additionally, it could have severe impacts on human health and economies. Thus, it's important to take actions to reduce the impacts of climate change.

Man is not the architect but the destroyer of the planet?

Humans have certainly had a significant impact on the planet through activities such as deforestation, pollution, and greenhouse gas emissions.

These activities have led to a range of environmental problems, including climate change, loss of biodiversity, and degradation of air and water quality. However, it's also important to note that humans have the capacity to be stewards of the planet as well.

Through responsible resource management, conservation, and the development and implementation of sustainable technologies, we can mitigate the negative impacts of human activity and work towards preserving the planet for future generations.

Current and projected impacts on different regions of the world

Climate change has the potential to affect different regions of the world in unique ways. Some of the current and projected impacts include:

In Arctic and boreal regions, warming temperatures are causing the permafrost to thaw and releasing stored carbon, which can exacerbate global warming.

Warming temperatures are also causing the loss of sea ice and threatening the survival of indigenous communities and animals such as polar bears.

In coastal regions, sea level rise and more intense storms are increasing the risk of flooding and storm surges, which can damage infrastructure and displace people.

In dry and semi-arid regions, such as the Mediterranean, climate change is expected to cause more frequent and severe droughts, which will negatively impact agriculture and water resources.

In tropical regions, warming temperatures and changes in precipitation patterns are expected to increase the incidence of diseases such as malaria and dengue fever.

In mountain regions, warming temperatures are causing the retreat of glaciers and threatening the water resources on which many communities depend.

Climate change is also expected to have disproportionate impacts on low-income and marginalized communities, as well as people living in developing countries which are less able to adapt to the impacts of climate change.

Desertification is a process of land degradation that occurs in arid, semi-arid, and dry sub-humid regions as a result of various factors, including climate change. The Intergovernmental Panel on Climate Change (IPCC) defines desertification as "land degradation in arid, semi-arid, and dry sub-humid areas resulting from various factors, including climatic variations and human activities."

The current global deserts due to climate change include regions such as the

Sahara Desert, which has been expanding southward in recent decades, and the Gobi Desert in China and Mongolia, which is also expanding. The Sahel region of Africa is also experiencing desertification, with increasing droughts, land degradation, and loss of vegetation.

Other areas affected by desertification due to climate change include parts of Australia, South America, and Asia. In these regions, prolonged droughts, rising temperatures, and changes in rainfall patterns are leading to soil erosion, loss of vegetation, and reduced agricultural productivity.

It is important to note that desertification is a complex process that is often caused by a combination of natural and human factors. While climate change is a major contributor, other factors such as overgrazing, deforestation, and unsustainable land use practices also play a significant role.

Climate change is having a wide range of effects on the planet, including both direct and indirect impacts. Some of the most significant current global effects due to climate change include:

1. Rising global temperatures: The average global temperature has increased by about 1°C since the pre-industrial era. This has led to a wide range of impacts, including melting glaciers and sea ice, rising sea levels, and more frequent and severe heatwaves.
2. Changes in precipitation patterns: Climate change is altering global precipitation patterns, leading to more frequent and severe droughts in some regions and more intense rainfall events in others. This can lead to more frequent and severe floods, landslides, and other natural disasters.
3. Ocean acidification: As the concentration of carbon dioxide in the atmosphere increases, the oceans are

becoming more acidic. This is having a range of impacts on marine life, including damaging coral reefs and reducing the ability of some organisms to build shells or skeletons.

4. Loss of biodiversity: Climate change is causing shifts in the ranges and behavior of many species, leading to declines in biodiversity. This can have cascading impacts on ecosystems and human well-being.

5. Increased frequency and severity of extreme weather events: Climate change is making many types of extreme weather events, such as hurricanes, floods, and wildfires, more frequent and severe.

6. Economic impacts: Climate change is already having significant economic impacts, including losses from extreme weather events, damage to infrastructure, and declines in agricultural productivity.

These are just a few of the many current global effects of climate change. As the planet continues to warm, it is likely that we will see even more severe and widespread impacts in the future.

Climate change is affecting regions around the world, but some areas are experiencing more severe impacts than others. Here are some of the regions that are currently being affected by climate change:

1. Arctic: The Arctic is experiencing some of the most rapid and severe impacts of climate change, including melting sea ice, thawing permafrost, and changing ecosystems.
2. Small island states: Small island states, such as the Maldives and Kiribati, are particularly vulnerable to sea level rise, which is already threatening their very existence.
3. Sub-Saharan Africa: Sub-Saharan Africa is experiencing more frequent and severe droughts, which are leading to

food and water shortages, as well as displacement of populations.

4. Southeast Asia: Southeast Asia is experiencing more frequent and severe heatwaves, which are putting people's health at risk, as well as exacerbating air pollution.

5. Coastal regions: Coastal regions around the world are already experiencing the impacts of sea level rise and more frequent and severe storms, which are leading to flooding, erosion, and damage to infrastructure.

6. High altitude regions: High altitude regions, such as the Himalayas and Andes, are experiencing melting glaciers, which are leading to reduced water supplies for millions of people.

These are just a few examples of the regions that are currently being affected by climate change. It's important to note that every region is unique, and the impacts of climate change will vary depending on a range of factors, including geography, culture, and socioeconomic conditions.

Hurricanes and cyclones are natural weather phenomena that have been occurring for millions of years. However, climate change is contributing to changes in the frequency, intensity, and impact of these storms in several ways.

1. Warmer sea surface temperatures: Hurricanes and cyclones form over warm ocean waters, and as the Earth's atmosphere warms due to climate change, sea surface temperatures are also rising. Warmer waters provide more energy for these storms to form and strengthen, leading to more frequent and intense hurricanes and cyclones.
2. Changing atmospheric conditions: Climate change is also altering atmospheric conditions that contribute to the formation and intensity of these storms. For example, changes in wind

patterns can create more favorable conditions for storm formation and intensification.

3. Rising sea levels: As the Earth's atmosphere warms, glaciers and ice caps are melting, and sea levels are rising. This means that hurricanes and cyclones that make landfall are more likely to cause flooding and damage in coastal regions.

4. Increased precipitation: Climate change is also leading to changes in precipitation patterns, with some regions experiencing more frequent and severe rainfall events. This can increase the risk of flooding and landslides during hurricanes and cyclones.

Overall, while hurricanes and cyclones are not new phenomena, climate change is making them more frequent, intense, and destructive. This underscores the urgent need to address the root causes of climate change and take steps to reduce greenhouse gas emissions and adapt to the changing climate.

Hurricanes and cyclones can occur in many regions of the world, but some areas are more prone to these storms than others. Regions that are particularly vulnerable to the impacts of hurricanes and cyclones include:

1. The Caribbean: The Caribbean is one of the most hurricane-prone regions of the world, with many island nations and coastal regions at risk of devastating storms.
2. The Gulf Coast of the United States: The Gulf Coast of the United States is also at high risk for hurricanes and cyclones, with major storms like Hurricane Katrina and Hurricane Harvey causing significant damage in recent years.
3. South and Southeast Asia: Many countries in South and Southeast Asia, including India, Bangladesh, and the Philippines, are vulnerable to cyclones,

which can cause significant damage and loss of life.

4. The Pacific Islands: Many small island nations in the Pacific, such as Samoa and Fiji, are at risk of cyclones, which can cause devastating impacts on their infrastructure and economies.

5. East Africa: Parts of East Africa, including Madagascar, Tanzania, and Mozambique, are at risk of tropical cyclones, which can cause significant flooding and damage.

These are just a few examples of the regions that are subject to the impacts of hurricanes and cyclones. As the climate continues to change, it is likely that we will see shifts in the frequency, intensity, and impacts of these storms, which will have significant implications for the people and ecosystems in these regions.

CHAPTER 2

GREENHOUSE GASES AND CLIMATE CHANGE

Greenhouse gases are gases in the Earth's atmosphere that trap heat and warm the planet. The primary greenhouse gases are water vapor, carbon dioxide (CO_2), methane (CH_4), nitrous oxide (N_2O) and ozone (O_3).

The most important of these gases is CO_2, which is responsible for about 60-80% of the greenhouse effect.

Human activities, such as burning fossil fuels, deforestation, and agriculture, have significantly increased the concentration of greenhouse gases in the atmosphere.

This has led to an increase in the Earth's average surface temperature, a phenomenon known as global warming. This warming has led to a number of climate change impacts, including rising sea levels, more frequent and severe heat waves, and changes in precipitation patterns.

The overwhelming scientific consensus is that the burning of fossil fuels and the associated increase in greenhouse gas concentrations in the atmosphere is the primary cause of recent global warming.

The Intergovernmental Panel on Climate Change (IPCC) has stated that it is extremely likely (greater than 95% probability) that human activities, particularly the burning of fossil fuels, are the dominant cause of the warming observed since the mid-20th century.

Role of carbon dioxide and other greenhouse gases warming the planet

Carbon dioxide (CO_2) is one of the primary greenhouse gases and plays a significant role in warming the planet.

When CO_2 and other greenhouse gases are released into the atmosphere, they trap heat and warm the planet, a phenomenon known as the greenhouse effect.

The burning of fossil fuels, such as coal, oil, and natural gas, is the primary source of CO_2 emissions. Deforestation and agriculture also contribute to CO_2 emissions by removing carbon-absorbing trees and creating land-use change.

The concentration of CO_2 in the atmosphere has been increasing since the Industrial Revolution, primarily due to human activities.

According to the Intergovernmental Panel on Climate Change (IPCC), the concentration of CO2 in the atmosphere has increased by about 45% since 1750, from about 280 parts per million (ppm) to over 414 ppm in 2020.

This increase in CO2 concentration is the primary driver of recent global warming, which has led to a number of climate change impacts.

In addition to CO2, other greenhouse gases such as methane, nitrous oxide, and chlorofluorocarbons also contribute to global warming.

Though these gases are present in smaller concentrations than CO2, they are much more effective at trapping heat, meaning that their warming impact per molecule is much stronger than CO2.

Sources of greenhouse gases emission

The primary sources of greenhouse gas emissions are:

Energy production: The burning of fossil fuels such as coal, oil, and natural gas for electricity and transportation is the largest source of greenhouse gas emissions. These activities release large amounts of carbon dioxide (CO_2) into the atmosphere.

Agriculture and deforestation: Activities such as clearing forests for agriculture, livestock production, and logging also contribute to greenhouse gas emissions.

Deforestation releases carbon stored in trees into the atmosphere and also reduces the ability of forests to absorb CO_2. Livestock production, particularly enteric fermentation in domesticated ruminants and manure management, are also significant sources of methane (CH_4) emissions.

Industrial processes: Industrial processes such as cement production, and certain chemical and metal manufacturing also emit greenhouse gases such as CO_2 and nitrous oxide (N_2O).

Waste: Landfills and waste treatment facilities are significant sources of methane emissions.

Transportation: Transportation, particularly the burning of fossil fuels in cars, buses, and airplanes also contributes to greenhouse gas emissions.

It's worth noting that different countries have different sources of greenhouse gas emissions, depending on their economic and energy structure.

For example, Developed countries tend to have more emissions from energy production and transportation, while developing countries might have more emissions from deforestation and agriculture.

Measuring and reducing emission

Measuring greenhouse gas emissions is important for understanding the sources of emissions and for setting reduction targets. There are several methods for measuring greenhouse gas emissions:

Inventory methods: National greenhouse gas inventories are the most commonly used method for measuring emissions at the country level. These inventories typically include data on emissions from energy production, transportation, agriculture, industrial processes, and waste. They are compiled using a combination of data from government sources, industry, and other stakeholders.

Remote sensing: Satellites and other remote sensing technologies can be used to measure emissions from specific sources such as power plants and large industrial facilities.

Top-down and bottom-up approaches: Top-down approaches involve measuring emissions by analyzing data on atmospheric concentrations of greenhouse gases and using mathematical models to estimate emissions. Bottom-up approaches involve measuring emissions directly at the source.

Once emissions have been measured, there are several ways to reduce them:

Energy efficiency and conservation: Improving energy efficiency in buildings and industry, as well as reducing energy consumption through conservation can help to reduce emissions.

Renewable energy: Increasing the use of renewable energy sources such as solar and wind power can reduce the need for fossil fuels and decrease emissions.

Carbon capture and storage: Carbon capture and storage (CCS) is a technology that captures CO2 emissions from power plants and industrial facilities before they are released into the atmosphere and stores them underground.

Carbon offsetting: Carbon offsetting is the practice of offsetting emissions by investing in projects that remove carbon from the atmosphere, such as reforestation and afforestation, agroforestry, soil carbon sequestration, sustainable land management and blue carbon.

Land-use change and forestry: Reducing deforestation, promoting afforestation and reforestation, as well as sustainable land management can help to remove carbon from the atmosphere and reduce emissions.

Clean transportation: Encourage the use of electric vehicles, public transportation, and other low-emission transportation options can help to reduce emissions.

It's worth noting that a reducing greenhouse gas emission is a global effort and that all countries have to work together to achieve significant reductions. International agreements such as the Paris Agreement provide a framework for countries to work together to reduce emissions and mitigate the impacts of climate change.

CHAPTER 3

CLIMATE CHANGE MITIGATION

Climate change mitigation refers to actions taken to reduce or prevent the emission of greenhouse gases, which contribute to global warming and climate change.

These actions can include increasing the use of renewable energy sources, improving energy efficiency, and implementing policies such as carbon taxes or cap-and-trade systems.

Mitigation can also include activities such as reforestation and soil carbon sequestration, which can remove carbon dioxide from the atmosphere.

The goal of mitigation is to slow or stop the increase of global temperatures and minimize the impacts of climate change.

Policies and technologies for reducing greenhouse gas emission

There are several policies and technologies that can be used to reduce greenhouse gas emissions and mitigate climate change. Some examples include:

Renewable energy sources such as solar, wind, and hydroelectric power, which do not produce greenhouse gas emissions during operation.

Energy efficiency measures such as building insulation, LED lighting, and efficient appliances, which can reduce the amount of energy needed to heat, cool, and power buildings and homes.

Carbon pricing, such as a carbon tax or cap-and-trade system, which puts a price on carbon emissions and provides an economic incentive for reducing them.

Carbon capture and storage (CCS), which captures carbon dioxide emitted by power plants and other industrial processes before it is released into the atmosphere and then stores it underground or in other long-term storage locations.

Electric vehicles, which emit less greenhouse gas than gasoline-powered vehicles, and also can be powered by renewable energy sources.

Reforestation and afforestation, which can remove carbon dioxide from the atmosphere by storing carbon in trees and other vegetation.

Sustainable Agriculture, which can decrease greenhouse gas emissions and increase carbon sequestration on farm land.

Building codes and regulations that encourage the use of energy-efficient materials, appliances and construction practices.

These are some of the policies and technologies that can be implemented to reduce greenhouse gas emissions; however, the most effective solution for reducing emissions is to reduce consumption.

CHAPTER 4
CLIMATE CHANGE ADAPTATION

Climate change adaptation refers to actions taken to prepare for and adjust to the impacts of climate change. These actions can include building sea walls and other infrastructure to protect against rising sea levels and increased storm surges, developing drought-resistant crops and water management strategies to cope with changing precipitation patterns, and creating early warning systems for extreme weather events.

Adaptation also includes planning and management strategies such as zoning and land-use planning, and building codes and standards, which can reduce the risks and impacts of extreme weather events on communities and infrastructure.

Adaptation strategies can also include ecosystem-based approaches such as protecting wetlands, restoring natural coastal buffers, and preserving biodiversity which can provide natural protection against extreme weather events and help to maintain ecosystem services.

Adaptation is a complex and ongoing process that should be integrated into decision-making at all levels, from the local to the international.

It requires collaboration between different sectors and stakeholders, and a clear understand0ing of the potential impacts of climate change on a particular region or community.

The adaptations in vulnerable sector such as agriculture and coastal areas

There are several adaptations that can be made in vulnerable sectors such as agriculture and coastal areas to mitigate the effects of climate change.

In agriculture, one adaptation strategy is to shift to crop varieties that are more tolerant to extreme weather conditions, such as drought or heat. Another strategy is to implement precision farming techniques that use weather data and other information to optimize crop yields.

In coastal areas, one adaptation strategy is to build sea walls or other types of coastal defenses to protect against sea level rise and storm surge. Another strategy is to promote managed retreat, which involves moving development away from vulnerable areas and protecting natural coastal habitats that can act as buffers against storm damage. Other strategies that can be used in both sectors include, water management, using drought-resistant plant varieties and early warning systems, and investing in infrastructure improvements.

The adaptation planning at the community and regional levels for climate change

Adaptation planning at the community and regional levels for climate change typically involves identifying and assessing the potential impacts of climate change on a specific area, and then developing and implementing strategies to reduce those impacts and increase resilience to the effects of climate change.

This can include measures such as developing early warning systems for extreme weather events, building more resilient infrastructure, protecting natural resources and ecosystems, and educating and engaging the community on the impacts of climate change and how to prepare for them.

Additionally, many communities and regions also work to reduce their greenhouse gas emissions as part of their adaptation planning, as reducing emissions can help to slow the rate of climate change and reduce the severity of future impacts.

CHAPTER 5

INT'L CLIMATE CHANGE AGREEMENTS

What are the International climate change agreements? The United Nations Framework Convention on Climate Change (UNFCCC) is an international treaty signed in 1992 that aims to stabilize greenhouse gas concentrations in the atmosphere to limit the magnitude of global warming and its negative impacts.

The treaty established the Conference of the Parties (COP) as the governing body of the UNFCCC and set the agenda for ongoing negotiations on reducing greenhouse gas emissions.

The 1997 Kyoto Protocol, which was adopted under the UNFCCC, is an international agreement that sets binding targets for 37 industrialized countries and the European Union for reducing greenhouse gas emissions.

The Paris Agreement, adopted in 2015 under the UNFCCC, aims to strengthen the ability of countries to deal with the impacts of climate change and to accelerate and intensify the actions and investments needed for a sustainable low carbon future.

The agreement aims to limit global warming to well below 2 degrees Celsius above preindustrial levels, with a goal of limiting warming to 1.5 degrees Celsius.

The history of international climate negotiation

The history of international climate negotiations dates back to the late 1980s, when scientists first began to raise concerns about the potential impacts of global warming caused by the burning of fossil fuels. In 1988, the Intergovernmental Panel on Climate Change (IPCC) was established by the United Nations to provide scientific assessments of the state of knowledge on climate change.

In 1992, the United Nations Framework Convention on Climate Change (UNFCCC) was adopted and signed by 154 countries, including the United States, during the Earth Summit in Rio de Janeiro.

The UNFCCC established a framework for international cooperation to stabilize greenhouse gas concentrations in the atmosphere in order to limit the magnitude of global warming and its negative impacts.

In 1997, the Kyoto Protocol was adopted under the UNFCCC, which set binding targets for 37 industrialized countries and the European Union for reducing greenhouse gas emissions. However, the United States, which is one of the largest emitters of greenhouse gases, did not ratify the protocol.

In the years that followed, negotiations continued under the UNFCCC, but progress was slow and limited, with countries failing to reach a comprehensive global agreement on emissions reduction.

In 2015, the Paris Agreement was adopted under the UNFCCC, which aims to limit global warming to well below 2 degrees Celsius above preindustrial levels, with a goal of limiting warming to 1.5 degrees Celsius.

The Paris Agreement was ratified by the United States under the Obama Administration but the Administration under Trump decided to withdraw from it.

Since the Paris Agreement, countries have been meeting regularly under the

UNFCCC to track progress and negotiate further actions to reduce emissions and adapt to the impacts of climate change.

However, the world is still not on track to achieve the goals of the Paris Agreement, and many experts believe that much more ambitious emissions reductions will be needed in order to avoid the worst impacts of climate change.

The Paris agreement and other development on climate change

The Paris Agreement, adopted in 2015 under the United Nations Framework Convention on Climate Change (UNFCCC), is a global agreement to combat climate change and to accelerate and intensify the actions and investments needed for a sustainable low carbon future.

The main objective of the Paris Agreement is to limit global warming to well below 2 degrees Celsius above preindustrial levels, with a goal of limiting warming to 1.5 degrees Celsius.

The Paris Agreement also includes provisions for countries to regularly report on their emissions and progress in reducing them, as well as provisions for developed countries to provide financial assistance to developing countries to help them reduce emissions and adapt to the impacts of climate change.

Since the Paris Agreement was adopted, countries have been meeting regularly under the UNFCCC to track progress and negotiate further actions to reduce emissions and adapt to the impacts of climate change. Some key developments on climate change since the Paris Agreement include:

The 2018 Intergovernmental Panel on Climate Change (IPCC) Special Report on Global Warming of 1.5°C, which found that limiting warming to 1.5 degrees Celsius above preindustrial levels is still possible, but would require immediate and unprecedented action.

The 2019 United Nations Climate Action Summit, where countries were urged to enhance their Nationally Determined Contributions (NDCs) under the Paris Agreement.

The increasing number of countries and cities around the world committing to net-zero emissions by mid-century or sooner.

The increasing number of businesses, investors and financial institutions committing to reducing emissions and aligning their strategies with the Paris Agreement.

The increasing number of countries and regions that are experiencing the impacts of climate change, such as sea level rise, heat waves, droughts and extreme weather events.

In summary, the Paris Agreement is considered as a key step forward in the global effort to address climate change, but much more ambitious actions are needed to achieve its goals and limit warming to 1.5 degrees Celsius.

Implementation and compliance challenges of climate change

Implementing policies to address climate change can present a variety of challenges, including:

Economic: The transition to a low-carbon economy can be costly, and some industries may be negatively affected.

Political: Climate change is a highly politicized issue, and there may be resistance to implementing certain policies.

Technological: Developing and deploying new technologies that reduce greenhouse gas emissions can be difficult and expensive.

International: Climate change is a global issue, and coordinating international action can be challenging.

Compliance challenges include:

1.   Lack of monitoring, reporting, and verification (MRV) systems

2.	Weak governance and institutions
3.	Limited capacity, particularly in developing countries
4.	Limited funding and investment
5.	Lack of public awareness and engagement.
6.	Lack of political will
7.	Resistance from corporate lobbies
	Lack of uniformity in regulations and policies across different countries.

CHAPTER 6

CLIMATE CHANGE AND SOCIETY

Climate change can have significant impacts on society, including:

1.   Environmental: Climate change can lead to sea level rise, more severe weather events, and changes in precipitation patterns, all of which can have devastating effects on natural systems and the ecosystems they support.

2. Economic: The impacts of climate change can disrupt industries and cause economic losses, particularly in sectors such as agriculture, forestry, and fishing.
3. Social: Climate change can exacerbate existing social inequalities and create new ones, particularly affecting vulnerable populations such as low-income communities and indigenous peoples.
4. Political: Climate change can lead to conflicts over resources, as well as put pressure on governments to implement policies to address the issue.
5. Health: Climate change can have a range of negative impacts on human health, including increased air pollution, the spread of disease, and more extreme weather events.
6. Migration: Climate change can lead to displacement of people from their homes due to rising sea levels, extreme weather events, droughts and flooding.
7. Food security: Climate change can affect food production in many ways, such as changes in temperature, precipitation and sea level,

which can lead to crop failure, soil degradation and loss of biodiversity.

8.   Biodiversity: Climate change can lead to declines in biodiversity, through changes in temperature, precipitation patterns, and sea level rise, which can lead to loss of habitats and extinction of species.

What are the social and economics dimension of climate change

Climate change has both social and economic dimensions. The social dimension of climate change refers to the impact that climate change has on people and communities, including issues such as displacement, health impacts, and access to resources.

The economic dimension of climate change refers to the impact that climate change has on the economy, including issues such as the cost of adaptation and mitigation, the effects on industries and sectors, and the potential for economic growth or decline.

Additionally, There is also the social cost of carbon, which refers to the economic damages caused by the emissions of one additional ton of carbon dioxide, including impacts on human health, property damage, and changes to ecosystems.

The political and policy responses to climate change

There are several political and policy responses to climate change, including:

Carbon pricing: This approach puts a price on carbon emissions, either through a carbon tax or a cap-and-trade system, to incentivize companies and individuals to reduce their emissions.

Renewable energy: Governments can support the development and deployment of renewable energy sources, such as solar and wind power, to reduce reliance on fossil fuels.

Energy efficiency: Policies can be implemented to improve the energy efficiency of buildings and appliances, reducing the overall demand for energy.

Electric vehicles: Governments can provide incentives to encourage the adoption of electric vehicles, which produce zero emissions while in operation.

Adaptation measures: Governments can also implement measures to help communities adapt to the effects of climate change that are already occurring or unavoidable.

International cooperation: Tackling climate change requires international cooperation to limit global greenhouse gas emissions and support for adaptation in developing countries.

Reforestation, afforestation and soil carbon sequestration: These are some of the ways to remove carbon from the atmosphere and store it in living biomass, dead wood, litter and soil.

It's worth to note that the most effective way to reduce emissions and slow climate change is to implement a combination of these responses.

The roles of civil society and grassroots action in respect of climate change

Civil society and grassroots action play important roles in addressing climate change. Some of these roles include:

Raising awareness: Civil society organizations and grassroots activists can raise awareness about the issue of climate change and its impacts on communities, particularly among marginalized groups.

Holding governments accountable: Civil society can monitor and hold governments accountable for their actions on climate change, including their compliance with international agreements and their domestic climate policies.

Advocating for policy change: Civil society groups can advocate for policies and regulations that address climate change, such as carbon pricing or increased investment in renewable energy.

Mobilizing citizens: Grassroots activists can mobilize citizens to take action on climate change, such as participating in protests and lobbying their elected representatives.

Providing solutions: Civil society organizations can provide solutions and best practices for addressing climate change, such as promoting sustainable development and sustainable land use.

Building coalitions: Civil society groups can build coalitions with other organizations and stakeholders, such as businesses and indigenous communities, to amplify their voices and increase their impact.

Impacting consumer behavior: Civil society organizations and grassroots movements can work to raise awareness on consumer behavior and its impact on climate change, and encouraging citizens to adopt more sustainable consumption patterns.

Overall, civil society and grassroots action can complement and support the efforts of governments and international organizations to address climate change, by bringing attention to the issue, pushing for more ambitious action, and developing and promoting innovative solutions.

CHAPTER 7

CLIMATE CHANGE: CAUSES AND EFFECTS

The long-term manifestations of weather and other atmospheric conditions in a given area or country, now usually represented by the statistical summary of its weather conditions during a period long enough to ensure that representative values are obtained (generally 30 years).

2. **Figuratively**; the context in general of a particular political, moral etc. situation.

3. **Obsolete**; an area of the earth's surface between two parallels of latitude.

There are many topics that can be discussed when considering the impacts of climate change on the environment and wildlife. Some possible topics include:

Rising sea levels: Climate change is causing the Earth's oceans to warm, which leads to the expansion of seawater and a rise in sea levels. This can threaten coastal habitats and the animals that live there.

Climate change can alter the temperature and precipitation patterns in different regions of the world. This can affect the types of plants and animals that can survive in those areas.

Extreme weather events: Climate change can increase the frequency and severity of extreme weather events, such as heatwaves, droughts, and storms. These events can have serious consequences for the environment and wildlife.

Habitat loss: As the climate changes, some animal species may need to migrate to new areas in order to survive. However, if their habitats are not protected, they may be unable to find suitable places to live.

Invasive species: Climate change can allow certain species to expand their ranges into areas where they were previously unable to survive. These invasive species can sometimes outcompete native species for resources and habitat, leading to declines in native species populations.

Pollution: Climate change can also lead to increases in air and water pollution, which can harm wildlife and the environment.

CHAPTER 8

BASIC QUESTIONS AND ANSWERS ON CLIMATE CHANGE

Climate change causes the rise in sea level through several mechanisms. One of the main causes is the thermal expansion of seawater as it warms. As the temperature of the ocean increases, the water molecules move faster and take up more space, leading to an increase in sea level.

Another cause of sea level rise is the melting of glaciers and ice sheets. As the Earth's temperature increases, glaciers and ice sheets are melting at an accelerated rate, adding water to the ocean and causing sea level to rise.

In addition, the loss of ice from the Greenland and Antarctic ice sheets also contributes to sea level rise. As the ice sheets melt and break off into the ocean, they add water to the ocean and cause sea level to rise.

Climate change also causes changes in weather patterns, such as more intense storms and heavy precipitation, which can lead to coastal flooding and erosion. This can further exacerbate the effects of sea level rise, making coastal areas more vulnerable to flooding and erosion.

Overall, climate change is one of the main drivers of sea level rise, and the effects are likely to continue in the future as the Earth's temperature continues to rise.

How do changes in temperature and precipitation affect climate change?

Changes in temperature and precipitation are closely linked to climate change. The Earth's temperature has been steadily rising due to increasing levels of greenhouse gases in the atmosphere. These gases trap heat and cause the Earth's temperature to rise, leading to changes in weather patterns, such as higher temperatures and increased precipitation.

The increased temperatures can lead to the melting of ice and snow, which contributes to sea level rise and changes in regional weather patterns. It also causes more droughts and heat waves in some regions, which leads to an increased risk of wildfires and water scarcity.

Changes in precipitation patterns can also lead to more intense storms and heavy rainfall in some regions, causing flooding and landslides. It can also lead to drought in other regions, which can affect agriculture and water availability.

Overall, changes in temperature and precipitation are closely linked to climate change and can have significant impacts on natural systems and human societies. These changes can further exacerbate the effects of climate change, making it more difficult for humans to adapt to the changing climate.

How does climate change result in extreme weather events?

Climate change results in extreme weather events due to the increase in greenhouse gas concentrations in the atmosphere, which causes the Earth's temperature to rise.

This increase in temperature leads to changes in weather patterns, including more frequent and severe heat waves, droughts, and heavy precipitation events. As the atmosphere becomes warmer, it holds more moisture, leading to more intense and frequent rain and snowfall events. This can result in flooding and landslides. Additionally, warmer ocean temperatures can lead to stronger and more frequent hurricanes and typhoons.

Overall, climate change leads to an increase in the frequency and intensity of extreme weather events, which can have severe impacts on human populations and natural ecosystems.

Is the depletion of ozone layer responsible for climate change?

The depletion of the ozone layer is not directly responsible for climate change, but it is related to it. The ozone layer is located in the stratosphere and protects the Earth from harmful ultraviolet radiation.

The depletion of the ozone layer is caused by the release of certain chemicals, such as chlorofluorocarbons (CFCs), which damage the ozone molecules.

Climate change, on the other hand, is caused by the increase of greenhouse gases, such as carbon dioxide, methane, and nitrous oxide, in the atmosphere. These gases trap heat and cause the Earth's temperature to rise. The main source of these gases is human activities, such as burning fossil fuels, deforestation, and agriculture.

However, the depletion of the ozone layer and climate change are related in that they are both caused by human activities that release harmful chemicals into the atmosphere.

The same activities that lead to the depletion of the ozone layer, such as the release of CFCs, also contribute to climate change by releasing greenhouse gases. Additionally, the depletion of the ozone layer can exacerbate the effects of climate change, as it can lead to more intense ultraviolet radiation reaching the Earth, which can cause damage to plants, animals, and human health.

Does climate change cause habitat loss?

Climate change can cause habitat loss in a number of ways. Rising temperatures can alter the range and distribution of certain species, making it difficult for them to find suitable habitats. Changes in precipitation patterns and increased frequency of extreme weather events can also impact the availability of water and other resources, leading to habitat loss.

Another way that climate change can cause habitat loss is through the acceleration of sea level rise, which can flood and erode coastal habitats and wetlands, making them uninhabitable for many species. Additionally, thawing permafrost and melting glaciers can also destroy or alter habitats, such as the tundra, that are home to many unique and sensitive species.

Climate change also indirectly affects the habitat through the increased wildfire and pest outbreak. Warmer and drier conditions promote the frequency and severity of wildfires, which can destroy large areas of forest and other habitats. Pest outbreak can also decimate tree populations in a forest, altering the structure and composition of the ecosystem.

Overall, climate change can have a wide range of negative impacts on habitats and the species that depend on them, making it an important area of concern for conservation efforts.

Can climate change cause pollution in the environment?

Climate change can indirectly cause pollution in the environment. For example, as the earth's temperature increases, it can lead to more intense storms and natural disasters, which can damage infrastructure and cause spills and leaks of pollutants.

Additionally, as sea levels rise, saltwater can intrude into freshwater sources, making them undrinkable and killing off fish and other aquatic life. Additionally, climate change can cause changes in weather patterns that can lead to an increase in wildfires, which can release pollutants into the air.

Can Climate change indirectly contribute to the spread of invasive species?

Yes, climate change can indirectly contribute to the spread of invasive species by altering the range and distribution of native species, creating new opportunities for non-native species to establish themselves. This can happen through a variety of mechanisms, such as changes in temperature and precipitation patterns, sea level rise, and increased frequency and intensity of extreme weather events. Additionally, climate change can also exacerbate existing problems associated with invasive species, such as increasing their reproductive success and enabling them to spread to new areas.

Is there hope of restoring the climate?

There is hope of restoring the climate, but it will require significant efforts from governments, organizations, and individuals to reduce greenhouse gas emissions and implement measures to sequester carbon.

This may include transitioning to clean energy sources, implementing carbon pricing, and investing in reforestation and land management practices.

Additionally, it will also require collective action and cooperation among nations to address the global nature of climate change.

What are those possibilities to restore climate?

There are several possibilities for restoring the climate, some of which include:

1. Reducing greenhouse gas emissions: This can be done by transitioning to clean energy sources such as wind, solar, and hydro power, as well as implementing measures to improve energy efficiency.
2. Carbon pricing: This involves placing a price on carbon emissions, which creates an economic incentive for individuals and companies to reduce their emissions.
3. Carbon sequestration: This involves removing carbon dioxide from the atmosphere and

storing it in long-term sinks such as forests, soils, and oceans.

4. Reforestation and afforestation: Planting trees and forests can absorb and store large amounts of carbon.

5. Sustainable land management: This includes practices such as agroforestry, conservation agriculture and sustainable livestock management, which can sequester carbon in soils and vegetation.

6. Investing in new technologies: Developing new technologies, such as direct air capture, that can remove CO2 from the atmosphere, and carbon utilization technologies that convert CO2 into valuable products.

7. Adaptation: Preparing for and adapting to the inevitable impacts of climate change, such as sea level rise and more frequent extreme weather events.

8. Education and awareness rising: Encouraging individuals and communities to understand and take action to address climate change.

It is important to note that these solutions are not mutually exclusive, but rather complementary and need to be implemented together in a comprehensive and coordinated manner.

Which continents are the greatest offenders in climate change?

It is difficult to point to a specific continent as the "greatest offender" in climate change as the issue is a global problem that affects all countries. However, developed countries, such as those in North America, Europe, and some countries in Asia, have historically had higher per capita greenhouse gas emissions due to their industrialized economies and high levels of consumption.

Developed countries have also been the largest emitters of greenhouse gases over the past century, whereas developing countries are expected to be the largest emitters in the future as their economies continue to grow.

However, it is also important to note that the responsibility for climate change is not limited to specific continents or countries, and that developed countries have a greater historical responsibility to take action to address the problem.

To what extend can technology improve the deteriorating effect of climate change?

Technology can play a significant role in improving the effects of climate change by reducing greenhouse gas emissions and increasing carbon sequestration. Some examples of how technology can be used to address climate change include:

1.   Renewable energy: Technologies such as wind turbines, solar panels, and hydroelectric power can provide clean and sustainable energy sources, reducing the need for fossil fuels.

2.   Energy storage: Battery storage and other technologies can help to store renewable energy, making it more reliable and available when it is needed most.

3.   Carbon capture: Technologies such as carbon capture and storage (CCS) and direct air capture (DAC) can remove carbon dioxide

from the atmosphere, reducing the overall concentration of greenhouse gases.

4.   Green transportation: Electric cars and other electric vehicles, as well as public transportation systems can reduce emissions from transportation.

5.   Smart grid: Smart grid technologies that optimize the use and distribution of energy can help to reduce energy waste and improve efficiency.

6. Sustainable agriculture: Precision agriculture, agroforestry, conservation agriculture and sustainable livestock management are practices that can help reduce emissions from agriculture and sequester carbon in soils and vegetation.

7. Carbon utilization: Technologies that convert CO2 into valuable products such as fuels, chemicals, and building materials can help to reduce emissions while creating new economic opportunities.

8. Adaptation: Technology can be used to help adapt to the impacts of climate change, such as sea-level rise, by creating early warning

systems, and building infrastructure that is more resilient to extreme weather events.

It is important to note that technology alone is not a solution to climate change; it must be combined with policies, regulations, and social changes to have significant impact.

The air pollution in certain cities has resulted in climate change, how is this true?

Air pollution, particularly in urban areas, is a major contributor to climate change. This is because many of the same activities that cause air pollution also release greenhouse gases, which trap heat in the atmosphere and contribute to global warming.

One of the main sources of air pollution in cities is the burning of fossil fuels, such as coal, oil, and natural gas, for transportation and energy generation. These fuels release pollutants such as carbon monoxide, sulfur dioxide, nitrogen oxides and particulate matter, which can harm human health, and also release carbon dioxide (CO_2) and other greenhouse gases which contribute to the warming of the planet.

Another source of air pollution in cities is the release of methane, a potent greenhouse gas, from landfills, agriculture, and waste management. The agriculture sector is also a significant contributor to air pollution through the application of fertilizers and pesticides that release pollutants and contribute to the formation of smog.

In addition, urbanization and land-use change can also contribute to climate change by reducing the amount of vegetation and increasing heat absorption in urban areas, leading to a phenomenon known as the urban heat island effect.

Reducing air pollution in cities can help to slow the rate of climate change by decreasing the amount of greenhouse gases released into the atmosphere and also improve the overall air quality and health of the citizens.

The use of fossil fuel is also a contributor to climate change, is it true?

Yes, the use of fossil fuels is a major contributor to climate change. Fossil fuels, such as coal, oil, and natural gas, are non-renewable resources that release large amounts of carbon dioxide (CO_2) and other greenhouse gases when they are burned to produce energy. These gases trap heat in the atmosphere, leading to an increase in global temperatures, which is referred to as global warming.

Fossil fuels are used for a variety of purposes, including electricity generation, transportation, and industrial processes. In addition to CO_2, the burning of fossil fuels also releases pollutants such as sulfur dioxide, nitrogen oxides, and particulate matter, which can harm human health and the environment.

According to the Intergovernmental Panel on Climate Change (IPCC), the burning of fossil fuels is responsible for about 78% of total greenhouse gas emissions. The majority of these emissions come from the burning of coal, oil, and gas for electricity and heat. The transportation sector is also a significant contributor, due to the burning of fossil fuels in cars, trucks, airplanes, and ships.

Reducing the use of fossil fuels and transitioning to cleaner energy sources, such as renewable energy, can help to slow the rate of climate change by decreasing the amount of greenhouse gases released into the atmosphere.

The use of greener energy or electricity can help to improve the effects of climate change by reducing greenhouse gas emissions. Green energy sources, such as solar, wind, and hydro power, do not release any carbon dioxide or other pollutants into the atmosphere when they generate electricity. In contrast, fossil fuels, such as coal, oil, and natural gas, release large amounts of greenhouse gases when they are burned to produce energy.

Transitioning to renewable energy sources can also help to reduce air pollution, which can have a positive impact on human health and the environment. Additionally, increasing the use of green energy can create jobs in the renewable energy sector and boost economic growth.

However, it's important to note that simply switching to renewable energy sources is not enough to completely solve the climate change problem, it needs to be combined with energy efficiency measures, carbon pricing, and also other efforts to sequester carbon.

Also, it is important to note that, although renewable energy sources don't emit greenhouse gases during the energy production process, the manufacturing, transportation, and installation of renewable energy systems also have an environmental impact, and should be taken into consideration.

In summary, increasing the use of green energy is an important step in addressing climate change, but it is just one of many actions that need to be taken to effectively address the problem.

Name these greener energy sources?

There are several types of green energy sources that can be used to generate electricity and reduce greenhouse gas emissions:

1. Solar power: This includes the use of solar panels to convert the sun's energy into electricity.
2. Wind power: This includes the use of wind turbines to convert the energy of the wind into electricity.
3. Hydroelectric power: This includes the use of the kinetic energy of falling water to generate electricity, through hydroelectric dams and small hydro systems.
4. Geothermal power: This includes the use of heat from the earth to generate electricity.

5. Biomass power: This includes the use of organic matter, such as wood, crops, and waste, to generate electricity through combustion or conversion into biogas.
6. Tidal power: This includes the use of the kinetic energy of tides to generate electricity
7. Wave power: This includes the use of the kinetic energy of waves to generate electricity.
8. Ocean thermal energy conversion (OTEC): This includes the use of the temperature difference between the surface and the depths of the ocean to generate electricity.

It is important to note that some of these sources may be more suitable for certain regions or applications than others. Additionally, it is also important to consider the environmental and social impacts of these sources, as well as the cost and feasibility of implementation.

Africa has a lot of sunshine almost all the year round, what are the governments in this region doing to harness this energy source?

Many African countries have abundant solar resources and have the potential to generate a significant amount of electricity from solar power. In recent years, governments in the region have taken steps to harness this energy source through a variety of initiatives, such as:

1.   Solar power projects: Many governments have implemented or are in the process of implementing large-scale solar power projects, such as photovoltaic (PV) power plants, to generate electricity for the grid.
2.   Mini-grid and off-grid systems: Governments have also been promoting the development of small-scale, mini-grid and off-grid solar systems to provide electricity to rural and remote areas where access to the grid is limited.
3.   Net metering and feed-in tariffs: Some governments have introduced policies and incentives, such as net metering and feed-in tariffs, to encourage individuals and

businesses to invest in solar power and connect to the grid.

4.   Solar energy education: Many governments have also invested in education and awareness raising programs to educate the public about the benefits and potential of solar energy.

5.   Private sector engagement: Governments in Africa have also increasingly been engaging the private sector to invest in the solar industry, through public-private partnerships and other schemes.

6.   International cooperation: African countries have also been seeking international cooperation and support to develop solar power, through initiatives such as the Africa Renewable Energy Initiative (AREI) and the Scaling Solar program.

It's important to note that, despite these efforts, the development of solar power in Africa still faces challenges such as lack of funding, lack of regulation and policy consistency, lack of technical capacity and infrastructure, and lack of political will.

However, there are many initiatives and organizations working to overcome these challenges and accelerate the deployment of solar energy across the continent.

The world is suffering from the effect of climate change because of lack of or inadequate initiative?

The world is suffering from the effects of climate change because of a lack of adequate action to address the problem. Despite an increase in awareness about the issue and the potential consequences, global greenhouse gas emissions continue to rise and many countries have not yet taken the necessary steps to reduce emissions and adapt to the impacts of climate change.

Are there reasons for this lack of action?

1.   Political will: Climate change is a complex and long-term problem that requires significant investments and policy changes, which can be difficult to secure in

the face of competing political priorities and short-term electoral cycles.

2.   Economic considerations: Transitioning to a low-carbon economy and investing in climate-resilient infrastructure can be costly, and some countries and industries may be reluctant to bear those costs.

3.   Lack of international cooperation: Climate change is a global problem that requires cooperation among nations to effectively address. However, international negotiations on climate change have been slow and difficult, and some countries have been reluctant to take on ambitious emissions reduction targets or provide financial assistance to developing countries.

4.   Misinformation and lack of public understanding: Climate change is a complex issue and some people may lack the knowledge or understanding of the science and potential impacts of the problem. Misinformation and disinformation can also spread confusion and mistrust among the public, making it harder to build support for action.

5.   Some countries and sectors are still heavily dependent on fossil fuels and have a difficulty in transitioning to cleaner energy sources.

To address these challenges and effectively address climate change, it will require a coordinated and ambitious global effort, involving strong political will, significant investments in clean energy and climate-resilient infrastructure, and international cooperation.

To what extend does nuclear reactor contribute to climate change?

Nuclear power, specifically the use of nuclear reactors, is considered by some to be a low-carbon energy source, as it does not produce greenhouse gases during the energy production process. However, it is important to consider the entire life-cycle of nuclear energy, including the mining and milling of uranium, the construction and operation of the reactor, the management of nuclear waste, and the decommissioning of the reactor.

During the operation of the reactor, nuclear power plants do not produce greenhouse gases, but the mining and milling of uranium, which is the fuel for the reactor, can have environmental impact. The construction and operation of the reactor also uses energy and materials, which can have an environmental impact.

The management of nuclear waste is another issue. Nuclear power plants produce radioactive waste, which is highly toxic and must be stored for thousands of years. This waste is difficult to store safely, and the long-term risks of leakage or accidents are significant.

Decommissioning of a reactor also requires a lot of energy and resources. It involves dismantling the reactor, dealing with the radioactive waste and restoring the site, which all requires energy and resources, and can have an environmental impact.

Overall, the contribution of nuclear energy to climate change is relatively small when compared to other energy sources. However, the risks and challenges associated with nuclear energy must be taken into account when assessing its role in addressing climate change. It is important to weigh the benefits and drawbacks of nuclear energy and consider it as one of the options in a portfolio of low-carbon energy sources that can help to reduce greenhouse gas emissions.

Which minerals mined are the greatest contributors to climate change?

The mining and extraction of certain minerals can contribute to climate change through several ways:

1.	Carbon emissions: The extraction and processing of some minerals, such as coal, oil, and natural gas, results in the release of large amounts of carbon dioxide (CO_2) and other greenhouse gases into the atmosphere.

2.	Deforestation: The mining of minerals such as gold, copper, and bauxite, often involves the clearing of large areas of forest, which can lead to the release of carbon stored in the trees and soil, as well as reducing the ability of forests to absorb CO2.

3.   Energy consumption: Extracting and processing minerals can be energy-intensive, and if the energy used in the process comes from fossil fuels, it can contribute to greenhouse gas emissions.

4.   Water consumption: Some mining operations consume large amounts of water, which can lead to water scarcity and impact on local communities, as well as altering local hydrology, which can affect the local climate.

5.   Emissions of other pollutants: Many mining operations also release pollutants such as sulfur dioxide, nitrogen oxides, and particulate matter into the air, which can harm human health and contribute to the formation of smog and acid rain.

Among these minerals, coal is considered to be the greatest contributor to climate change as it is responsible for the largest share of carbon emissions when burned. Oil and natural gas are also significant contributors to climate change, although the emissions from these sources are less than coal.

Deforestation or wildfire to what extend does it contribute climate change

Deforestation and wildfire can both contribute to climate change in several ways:

1.   Carbon emissions: Forests store large amounts of carbon in their trees, soil, and vegetation. When forests are destroyed by logging, clearing for agriculture or through wildfire, the carbon stored in them is released into the atmosphere, contributing to the warming of the planet. Deforestation is responsible for about 10-15% of global greenhouse gas emissions.

2.   Loss of carbon sequestration: Forests act as carbon sinks, absorbing and storing carbon from the atmosphere through photosynthesis. When forests are destroyed, they can no longer perform this function,

leading to an increase in atmospheric carbon levels.

3. Loss of biodiversity: Forests are home to a wide variety of plant and animal species, and their destruction can lead to the loss of biodiversity and ecosystem services.

4. Altering local hydrology: Forests play an important role in regulating local hydrology, influencing precipitation and stream flow. Their destruction can lead to changes in local water cycles, which can affect the local climate.

5. Indirect effects: Deforestation and wildfire can also have indirect effects on climate change through their impact on the livelihoods and well-being of local communities, leading to increased pressure on remaining natural resources and potentially contributing to migration and conflict.

Wildfire, in particular, can have a significant impact on climate change. Wildfires release large amounts of carbon stored in trees and soil into the atmosphere, and also contribute to the formation of black carbon and other pollutants that can have a warming effect on the planet. In addition, wildfires can also destroy carbon sinks, leading to a loss of carbon sequestration and a reduction in biodiversity.

To what level can mankind save the flora and fauna on the earth?

Mankind has the ability to take significant steps to protect and conserve the flora and fauna on Earth, but it will require a concerted and sustained effort. Some ways that mankind can help to save the flora and fauna include:

1. Reducing deforestation and promoting reforestation: Reducing the rate of deforestation and promoting reforestation can help to protect and restore habitats for plants and animals, and also help to mitigate climate change by sequestering carbon.

2. Implementing conservation measures: Governments, organizations, and individuals can take a number of measures to protect and

conserve wildlife and their habitats, such as creating protected areas, implementing hunting and fishing regulations, and controlling invasive species.

3. Sustainable use of natural resources: Mankind can use natural resources in a more sustainable way, by reducing overconsumption, improving the efficiency of resource use and supporting the development of renewable resources

4. Climate change mitigation: Reducing greenhouse gas emissions and slowing the rate of climate change can help to protect many species and their habitats, by keeping global temperatures from rising to dangerous levels.

5. Support and invest in scientific research: Supporting and investing in scientific research can help to understand the impacts of human activities on wildlife and their habitats, as well as identifying and monitoring endangered species.

6. Raising awareness and education: Raising awareness and educating the public about the importance of conservation and the

consequences of environmental degradation can help to build support for conservation efforts.

It's important to note that conservation efforts alone are not enough, they need to be combined with policies, regulations and social changes to have a significant impact. Additionally, conservation efforts must also take into account the needs and well-being of local communities, and consider the social and economic factors that contribute to environmental degradation.

Advancement in technology is a major factor to climate change, can man do without technology?

Advancements in technology have contributed to climate change by increasing the amount of greenhouse gases released into the atmosphere and by altering the Earth's natural systems. However, technology also offers many solutions to address climate change and reduce greenhouse gas emissions.

It's not possible or practical to do without technology entirely, as technology plays a vital role in many aspects of modern life. However, it's important to use technology in a responsible and sustainable way to minimize its negative impacts on the environment.

One way to do this is by transitioning to cleaner and more efficient technologies. For example, renewable energy technologies such as solar and wind power can replace fossil fuels as a source of electricity. Electric vehicles can replace gasoline-powered cars, and energy-efficient appliances can reduce energy consumption in homes and buildings.

Another way is to use technology to reduce waste, conserve resources and minimize pollution. For example, recycling technologies can reduce the amount of waste going to landfills, and digital technologies can help to reduce the use of paper and other resources.

Additionally, technology can also be used to monitor and track the impacts of climate change, and to help communities and ecosystems adapt to the changes that are already taking place. For example, satellite imagery and remote sensing technologies can help to track changes in vegetation and land use, and weather forecasting models can help communities prepare for extreme weather events.

In conclusion, technology has played a major role in causing climate change, but it can also be an important tool in addressing the problem. It's important to use technology in a responsible and sustainable way to minimize its negative impacts and maximize its potential to reduce greenhouse gas emissions, conserve resources and help communities adapt to a changing climate.

What are the possible ways to produce a safer technology that will not have serious adverse effect on this planet?

There are several ways to produce safer technology that will not have serious adverse effects on the planet:

1.	Developing cleaner and more efficient technologies: Research and development can focus on creating new technologies that are less polluting and more energy-efficient. For example, renewable energy technologies such as solar and wind power, can replace fossil fuels as a source of electricity, and electric vehicles can replace gasoline-powered cars.

2.	Implementing sustainable design principles: New technologies can be designed with sustainability in mind, by using materials and resources in a more efficient way, and by minimizing waste and pollution.

3.	Incorporating life-cycle thinking: The entire life-cycle of a product or technology, from the extraction of raw materials to disposal or recycling, should be considered when designing new technologies, in order to minimize environmental impacts.

4.   Encouraging circular economy principles: Technologies can be designed and developed to enable the recovery and reuse of valuable materials and resources, and to minimize the generation of waste.

5.   Investing in research and development: Governments and private sector organizations can invest in research and development of safer technologies, including basic and applied research, demonstration projects and commercialization.

6.   Creating incentives and regulations: Governments can create policies and regulations that encourage the development and use of safer technologies, such as tax incentives, subsidies, and performance standards.

7.   Public education and awareness: Raising public awareness and education about the environmental impacts of technology and the benefits of safer technologies can help to create demand for these products and services.

It's important to note that, to produce safer technology that will not have serious adverse effects on the planet, it will require a multidisciplinary approach, and need to involve collaboration among governments, industry, academia and civil society.

How can effective education and awareness produce a positive result in climate change?

Effective education and awareness can produce a positive result in climate change in several ways:

1.   Increasing public understanding: Education and awareness raising campaigns can help to increase public understanding of the science of climate change, the potential impacts and the actions that can be taken to address the problem.

2.   Building support for action: By raising awareness and understanding of the issue, education and awareness campaigns can help to build support for action on climate change among the public and decision-makers.

3.   Encouraging behavior change: Education and awareness campaigns can encourage individuals, communities, and organizations to take action to reduce their greenhouse gas emissions, through changes in energy use, transportation, consumption, and waste management.

4.   Promoting sustainable development: Education and awareness campaigns can promote sustainable development by highlighting the benefits of low-carbon, resilient and inclusive development, and the need to ensure that development is consistent with the mitigation of climate change.

5.   Empowering individuals: By providing people with the knowledge and tools to understand and address the problem, education and awareness campaigns can empower individuals to take action on climate change, both in their personal and professional lives.

6.   Creating a sense of urgency: education and awareness can create a sense of urgency

and mobilize people to act quickly to address the problem.

7.   Fostering innovation: Education and awareness campaigns can foster innovation by highlighting the need for new technologies, policies, and practices that can help to reduce greenhouse gas emissions and adapt to the impacts of climate change.

It's important to note that, effective education and awareness campaigns should be targeted, inclusive and culturally appropriate, and involve a range of stakeholders, including government, civil society, private sector and local communities. Additionally, education and awareness campaigns should be integrated into broader climate change policies and actions.

To what extend does poor town planning procedure increase infect of climate change?

Poor town planning procedures can increase the impact of climate change in several ways:

1.   Urban heat island effect: Poor town planning can lead to the creation of urban heat islands, where urban areas are significantly warmer than surrounding rural areas. This can lead to increased energy consumption for cooling, as well as increased health risks for residents.

2.   Green space loss: Poor town planning can lead to the loss of green spaces and natural habitats, which can reduce the ability of urban areas to absorb and store carbon, as well as provide important ecosystem services such as pollination and pest control.

3.   Reduced resilience to extreme weather events: Poor town planning can lead to the development of vulnerable areas that are at high risk from extreme weather events such as floods, droughts, and heatwaves. This can result in increased damages and disruptions, as well as increased costs for emergency response and recovery.

4.   Inefficient use of resources: Poor town planning can lead to the inefficient use of resources such as water and energy, as well as

increased transportation emissions and congestion.

5. Limited opportunities for active transportation: Poor town planning can limit opportunities for active transportation such as walking and cycling, which can lead to increased reliance on cars and public transportation, resulting in more emissions and air pollution.

6. Reduced air quality: Poor town planning can also lead to increased air pollution and reduced air quality, as a result of increased traffic and industrial activities in urban areas.

Effective town planning can help to reduce the impacts of climate change by promoting low-carbon, energy-efficient, and resilient development, protecting and restoring natural habitats, and providing safe and accessible transportation options. It can also help to reduce the urban heat island effect, conserve resources, and improve the quality of life for residents.

Do issues of corruption in government and other organizations contribute to climate change?

Corruption in government and other organizations can contribute to climate change in several ways:

1.   Lack of effective policies and regulations: Corruption can lead to the weakening or non-enforcement of policies and regulations aimed at reducing greenhouse gas emissions and promoting sustainable development. This can result in increased emissions and a lack of progress in addressing climate change.

2.   Misuse of public funds: Corruption can lead to the misallocation or embezzlement of public funds that are intended for climate change mitigation and adaptation. This can reduce the resources available for effective action on climate change and also undermine public trust in government.

3.   Inefficient use of resources: Corruption can also lead to the inefficient use of

resources such as land, water, and energy, which can contribute to climate change.

4.   Environmental degradation: Corruption can lead to the illegal activities such as illegal logging, illegal mining and illegal hunting, which can lead to environmental degradation and biodiversity loss, both of which contribute to climate change.

5.   Unfair allocation of resource: Corruption can also lead to an unfair allocation of resources, such as carbon credits, which can result in the over-allocation of emissions allowances to certain industries or companies, while others are left to bear a disproportionate burden of emissions reductions.

6.   Lack of transparency: Corruption can also lead to a lack of transparency and accountability, making it difficult to track and measure progress on climate change, and making it easier for corrupt actors to hide their activities.

It's important to note that, combating corruption is crucial in order to ensure that policies and actions to address climate change are effective, fair and efficient, and that public trust and confidence in government and other organizations is maintained.

Is it true that the multinational oil companies are one of the major contributors to climate change?

Multinational oil companies are considered to be major contributors to climate change due to their production and sale of fossil fuels such as oil and natural gas. The burning of these fuels releases large amounts of greenhouse gases, primarily carbon dioxide (CO_2), into the atmosphere, which contributes to the warming of the planet.

According to various estimates, the burning of fossil fuels is responsible for around 80% of global greenhouse gas emissions. Oil companies are responsible for a significant proportion of these emissions, as they extract and refine oil and natural gas and sell it to be used as a primary energy source.

Additionally, oil and gas companies are responsible for emissions that occur during the exploration, extraction and production of fossil fuels, which can have a significant impact on local communities and the environment.

It's important to note that, some oil companies have taken steps to reduce their greenhouse gas emissions, such as investing in renewable energy, improving energy efficiency, and reducing flaring and venting of natural gas. However, it has been argued that these steps are not enough and that the oil and gas industry needs to transition to a low-carbon energy system in order to address the problem of climate change.

To what level does oil pollution increase climate change?

Oil pollution can increase climate change in several ways:

1.   Greenhouse gas emissions: Oil spills can lead to the release of large amounts of greenhouse gases such as methane, a potent greenhouse gas, into the atmosphere. This contributes to global warming and climate change.

2.   Loss of carbon sequestration: Oil spills can also damage and kill vegetation and wildlife, reducing the ability of ecosystems to absorb and store carbon, leading to an increase in atmospheric carbon levels.

3.   Loss of biodiversity: Oil spills can lead to the death of many plant and animal species, reducing biodiversity and the ability of ecosystems to provide important services such as pollination and pest control.

4.   Altering local hydrology: Oil spills can affect local water cycles, altering precipitation and stream flow, which can affect the local climate.

5.   Emissions of other pollutants: Oil spills can also release pollutants such as sulfur dioxide, nitrogen oxides, and particulate matter into the air, which can harm human

health and contribute to the formation of smog and acid rain.

6.   Effects on human and animal health: Oil spills can have a significant impact on human and animal health, by contaminating air, water and soil, and exposing people and wildlife to toxic chemicals.

Oil spills also have a significant impact on the environment and communities, and can lead to long-term damage to habitats and loss of biodiversity, as well as economic losses for local communities and industries, such as fishing and tourism.

It's important to note that, preventing and mitigating oil pollution can help to reduce the impacts of climate change, and that oil companies have a responsibility to take measures to prevent spills and to minimize the damage caused by spills when they do occur.

Are the compensations paid by these companies help to restore the damage environment?

Compensations paid by oil companies for environmental damage caused by oil spills and other pollution can help to restore the damaged environment to some extent, but it is not a guarantee and it depends on the amount of compensation, how it is used and the effectiveness of the restoration efforts.

Compensations can be used to fund cleanup and restoration efforts, such as removing oil from the shoreline and replanting vegetation, as well as compensate local communities and industries that have been affected by the spill.

However, it is important to note that, the effectiveness of the restoration efforts is dependent on a number of factors, such as the type and extent of the damage, the availability of suitable restoration techniques, and the ability of the affected ecosystems to recover. In some cases, the damage caused by an oil spill may be irreversible, and compensation alone may not be able to fully restore the environment.

Additionally, the amount of compensation paid by the companies may not be sufficient to cover the full costs of the cleanup and restoration efforts, and the affected communities may not be fully compensated for their losses.

It's important to note that, preventing oil pollution in the first place is the most effective way to protect the environment and should be the primary focus of companies and governments. This can be achieved through measures such as improving the safety and design of offshore oil drilling platforms, and implementing stricter regulations and penalties for oil spills.

Do advance countries pays deaf ear to environmental pollution when it affects developing countries?

It is possible that advanced countries may pay less attention to environmental pollution when it affects developing countries, for a number of reasons.

1.   Lack of political will: Developing countries may have less political influence on the global stage, and their concerns may not be given the same weight as those of advanced countries.

2.   Limited resources: Developing countries may have limited resources to address environmental pollution and may not have the same capacity to implement effective regulations or to fund cleanup and restoration efforts.

3.   Lack of access to information: Developing countries may not have the same access to information and technology to monitor and report on environmental pollution, which can make it harder to draw attention to the problem.

4.   Different priorities: Developing countries may have different priorities, such as economic development and poverty reduction, which may take precedence over addressing environmental pollution.

5.   Different cultural and social values: Advanced countries may have different

cultural and social values regarding environmental protection, and may not attach the same importance to environmental issues as developing countries.

It's important to note that, environmental pollution is a global problem that affects all countries, and that it is in the interest of all countries to work together to address it. Advanced countries should recognize the impact of environmental pollution on developing countries and support them in their efforts to address it. Additionally, the international community should work together to create global policies and regulations that help to reduce environmental pollution and support sustainable development.

More than 90% of environmental pollution emanates from activities of the advance countries,

It is true that a significant proportion of global environmental pollution can be attributed to activities of advanced countries. According to various estimates, advanced countries have historically been responsible for a large share of the world's greenhouse gas emissions, which is a major contributor to climate change.

Historically, the industrialized nations have been responsible for the majority of the emissions of greenhouse gases, which is responsible for the majority of climate change, while the emissions from the developing countries are increasing as they are catching up with the developed world in terms of economic growth and industrialization.

Additionally, advanced countries also have higher levels of consumption, which can lead to increased waste and pollution. The overconsumption of resources and the production of goods and services in advanced countries, can also lead to environmental degradation, deforestation and the loss of biodiversity in other parts of the world.

However, it's important to note that, while advanced countries may have contributed a large share of global environmental pollution, it is a problem that affects all countries, and that all countries must take responsibility for addressing it. Developing countries are also increasingly becoming major emitters and contributors to environmental pollution, and it is important for all countries to work together to reduce emissions and address the problem of environmental pollution.

CONCLUSION

Climate change is a complex and pressing issue that is caused by human activities such as the burning of fossil fuels, deforestation, and industrial processes. It is leading to rising temperatures, sea level rise, and more severe weather events, and has the potential to cause significant harm to human societies and ecosystems around the world. To address climate change, it is essential to reduce greenhouse gas emissions, transition to renewable energy sources, and invest in research and development of new technologies.

Additionally, policies and actions to adapt to the impacts of climate change, such as sea level rise, are also necessary. It is important to act now to address climate change and mitigate its impacts.

SUMMARY OF KEY FINDINGS AND RECOMMENDATIONS ON CLIMATE CHANGE

Climate change refers to the long-term changes in the Earth's climate, including temperature, precipitation, and weather patterns. The main cause of climate change is the burning of fossil fuels, which releases greenhouse gases, such as carbon dioxide, into the atmosphere. These gases trap heat from the sun, causing the Earth's temperature to rise.

Key findings of climate change research include:

The Earth's average surface temperature has risen about 1.8 degrees Fahrenheit (1 degree Celsius) since the late 1800s, with most of the warming occurring in the past few decades.

The burning of fossil fuels is the main cause of the increase in carbon dioxide and other greenhouse gases in the atmosphere.

The warming of the planet is causing more extreme weather events, such as heat waves, droughts, and heavy rainfall.

Sea levels are rising due to the melting of ice sheets and glaciers and the thermal expansion of the oceans.

Climate change is already having a significant impact on ecosystems and wildlife, and could lead to the extinction of many species.

The recommendations to address climate change include:

Reducing the burning of fossil fuels by increasing the use of renewable energy sources, such as solar and wind power.

Improving energy efficiency in buildings, transportation, and industry.

Planting trees and other vegetation to absorb carbon dioxide from the atmosphere.

Investing in research and development of new technologies to reduce emissions and adapt to the changing climate.

Encouraging individuals and organizations to reduce their own greenhouse gas emissions by conserving energy and making more sustainable choices.

International cooperation to mitigate and adapt to climate change.

It's important to note that Climate change is a complex and global issue that require immediate and collective actions to address.

References and suggested reading on climate change

There are many resources available for learning more about climate change and its impacts. Here are a few references and suggested readings that provide a good overview of the issue:

Intergovernmental Panel on Climate Change (IPCC) - The IPCC is a scientific body established by the United Nations to assess the state of climate change science. Their reports provide a comprehensive overview of the current state of the science and are widely considered to be the most authoritative source of information on climate change.

"Climate Change: The Science of Global Warming and Our Energy Future" by Joe Romm - This book provides a detailed explanation of the science of climate change and the potential impacts of global warming, as well as a discussion of the policy options available to address the problem.

"Climate Change and Society: Sociological Perspectives" edited by Riley E. Dunlap and Robert J. Brulle - This book provides a sociological perspective on climate change, examining the social and cultural factors that influence public perceptions of the issue and the political response to it.

"An Inconvenient Truth: The Planetary Emergency of Global Warming and What We Can Do About It" by Al Gore - This book and the accompanying film of the same name raise awareness about the causes and consequences of global warming, and call for immediate action to address the problem.

"Global Warming: Understanding the Forecast" by David Archer - This book provides a comprehensive overview of the science of global warming, including the causes, impacts, and potential solutions.

"Climate Change: A Very Short Introduction" by Mark Maslin - This book provides a concise overview of the science of climate change, its impacts, and the policy options available to address the problem.

It's important to note that the scientific understanding of climate change is constantly evolving, so it's important to stay informed about the latest research and developments.